IMAGES OF THE

DORSET COAST

by Roger Holman

DORSET BOOKS

First published in 1998 by Dorset Books
Reprinted 2000, 2001
Copyright © 1998 Roger Holman

ISBN 1 871164 60 5

British Library Cataloguing-in-Publication-Data
A CIP data record for this book is available from the British Library

DORSET BOOKS
Official Publisher to Dorset County Council
Halsgrove House
Lower Moor Way
Tiverton EX16 6SS
T: 01884 243242
F: 01884 243325
www.halsgrove.com

Printed and bound in Italy by
Centro Grafico Ambrosiano, Milan

Looking across the Frome to St Mary's Church, Wareham.

CONTENTS

FOREWORD

My interest in photography was sparked off in my teens when I came across an old copy of *Amateur Photographer* while clearing out a storeroom in the village youth club. A friend and I set up a darkroom and started to do our own processing, progressing later to audio-visual presentations. However, it is only since I passed the family retail electrical business over to two of my sons that I have had enough leisure time to take pictures for books, magazines and greetings cards. Fortunately, I have a very tolerant wife who doesn't complain if she finds I am missing when she wakes up in the morning!

Going back two generations, my family have all been born and bred in Dorset, so perhaps that is why I have had a lifelong love affair with this county and particularly with the coast. I am constantly drawn back to it, in all its moods, because there is nowhere else quite as magical for me. I cannot imagine what it must be like not to live near the sea.

Landscape photography is a frustrating business. To get really good pictures you have to be in the right place at the right time – generally when the weather and the light are at their most unpredictable – which often entails returning again and again to the same spot. This is not too difficult when the location is close to home, but a different matter when it's at the other end of the county. Nevertheless, the feeling of satisfaction experienced when that elusive picture is captured on film makes it all worth while.

When I was asked to produce this book, I felt excited and privileged. I hope my photographs convey a little of the magic of the Dorset coast and will tempt some of those who are unfamiliar with the area to go out, explore and enjoy it.

The technical details, for those who are interested: most of the pictures were taken with a 6 x 6 cm Bronica SQA and some with a 6 x 7 cm Mamiya RZ. A 5 x 4 Cambo Wide was used for the panoramics, and one or two shots were taken on a 35 mm Canon T90. The only filters I use are a Polarizer, an 81a Warm Up and very occasionally a Gray Grad. Fuji Provia was the film stock.

My thanks go to my wife Rosemary for her support and help with the text, and to Barry Miles for helping me choose the pictures.

INTRODUCTION

In 1965 Monica Hutchings wrote: 'Dorset is a small, modest but beautiful county which is not nearly so well known or appreciated as it deserves to be.' She went on to say: 'There are no motorways and the number of traffic lights can be counted on one hand.' Nearly thirty-five years later there are many more traffic lights but, suprisingly, not one motorway. Maybe this is what has helped keep Dorset 'not so well known'.

There are certain places that do become extremely busy during the summer but it is possible even then to walk for long periods along the coast without seeing another soul. And Charles II, who did his fair share of travelling before becoming king, said that he 'had never seen a finer county, either in England or out of it'. It is perhaps lucky that the really large conurbations of Bournemouth, Poole and Christchurch are on the eastern fringe, leaving most of the rest of the county largely undisturbed.

It is not surprising that the Dorset coast is internationally famous for its scenery: there is no other county in southern England that can boast such a variety of landscape, all within seventy-odd miles. It ranges from safe sandy beaches, which in the winter months are quite often completely deserted, to towering chalk and limestone cliffs, caves, coves and bays and the unique Chesil Beach, regarded by many as one of the wonders of the world. Then there are the harbours of Lyme Regis, Weymouth, Christchurch and of course Poole, which is the second largest natural harbour in the world, with an indented shoreline of over a hundred miles. It is a mecca for yachtsmen and windsurfers and supports a great deal of bird and marine life. In stark contrast is the bleak, windswept Isle of Portland, not pretty but with a definite character of its own. 'The Gibraltar of Wessex', Hardy named it.

Because of its unique geology much of the Dorset coast is now being considered as a World Heritage Site, an honour it would share with such places as the Grand Canyon.

Walking the coastal path, one is reminded that the shoreline is changing all the time (and will continue to do so), as it is constantly eroded by the sea, wind, and rain. The most dramatic instance of the effect of erosion was the 1839 landslip at Lyme, in which over forty acres of land dropped to a lower level, carrying fields and cottages with it. At Stair Hole, next to Lulworth Cove, the sea has broken through the Portland stone to form a smaller version of Durdle Door. The land behind is being eroded, as it is at the cove, and eventually the two will join. And while the beach at one end of Studland Bay is growing, it is in retreat at the other, so that the summer chalets there have had to be repositioned three times in recent years.

Smuggling has always played a large part in Dorset folklore, particularly on the coast. With its numerous isolated caves and coves, it provided an ideal operating area, aided by the fact that apart from the government no one considered smuggling a particularly heinous crime. Isaac Gulliver, one of the county's most audacious smugglers, led a band of fifty men dressed in a livery of frock coats and powdered hair who became known as the 'White Wigs'. Gulliver was never brought to book.

He ended his days as a wealthy and respected member of the community and was buried in a vault in Wimborne Minster.

In previous centuries, most of the population of Dorset were involved in fishing and in agriculture; the first stirrings of trade unionism began with six Dorset farm labourers, the Tolpuddle martyrs. The exceptions were the men who worked in the famous Portland and Purbeck quarries, quarrying stone that continues to be used all over the world and the Wareham ball clay shipped to Staffordshire to make high-grade pottery. ECC Ball Clays now excavate up to 200,000 tons annually.

The most valuable mineral found in Dorset is of course oil, which is still being pumped at Kimmeridge after nearly forty years and more recently at the oil well at Wytch Farm in Poole Harbour. As a whole, the field produces a total of 3,150,000 gallons of oil a day.

Until 1981 The National Trust owned a relatively small amount of land in Dorset, although with the aid of The Enterprise Neptune appeal and other bequests their holding was gradually being increased, but it was the massive bequest by Sir Ralph Bankes of over 16,000 acres, the largest the Trust had ever received, that turned it into the county's premier landholder. The Trust now owns more than 22,000 acres of land in Dorset, including some of the finest coast and countryside in Britain.

In addition to the County Council, The National Trust, The Dorset Wildlife Trust, The Royal Society for Protection of Birds and English Nature are all active in Dorset, helping to preserve the county's treasured landscape and wildlife for future generations to enjoy.

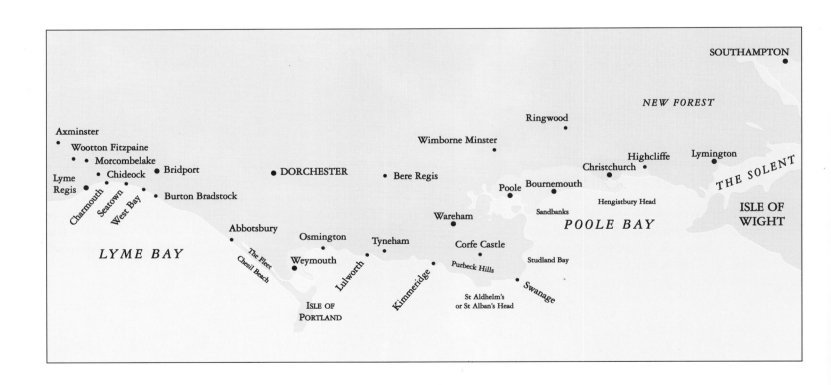

HIGHCLIFFE TO SANDBANKS

Highcliffe has marked the eastern boundary of Dorset since the 1970s, when changes in county boundaries transferred it, along with Mudeford, Christchurch and Bournemouth, from Hampshire to Dorset.

The Hampshire Avon and the Dorset Stour both end their journeys in Christchurch Harbour. The impossibility of any very large craft gaining entry into this haven is one factor that makes it a sanctuary for vast numbers of birds for whom the reeds and shallows are an ideal habitat.

On a clear day, from the 180-foot summit of Hengistbury Head there are magnificent views in every direction: the coast and Isle of Wight to the east, the harbour and the New Forest to the north and the Boscombe/Bournemouth coastline stretching down to the Purbecks in the west. On the eastern slopes of Hengistbury Head there is a small lake where ironstone was once excavated and transported to Bucklers Hard to be smelted down and made into fittings for the ships of Lord Nelson's fleet.

Although Bournemouth is arguably the largest town in Dorset and now boasts a university, two centuries ago it did not exist. Its origins date from 1810, when Captain Lewis Tregonwell, having fallen in love with the area while visiting it on holiday, built himself a house at the mouth of the little River Bourne. The safe beaches remain but tarmac and buildings have now replaced the huge expanses of sand dunes that stretched for miles inland and provided a haven for smugglers, especially the famous Gulliver, who claimed that no customs officer ever came to harm at his hand.

Sandbanks was regarded as a remote headland in 1897, when Guglielmo Marconi set up his 100-foot mast outside the Haven Hotel for his wireless telegraphy experiments. He could often be seen pacing the beach wearing an extraordinary 'helmet' – a set of headphones – as he tried to find a good spot to receive a signal.

From Evening Hill near Sandbanks there is a magnificent view of the harbour, which during the war was home to a Sunderland flying-boat squadron, but is now filled with yachts and cruisers.

Before sunrise is a good time to take a stroll along the beach at Highcliffe.

Early morning mist on the river at Christchurch.

Christchurch Harbour from Hengistbury Head.

Looking towards Highcliffe from Hengistbury.

Hengistbury Head.

View from Hengistbury Head towards Boscombe and Bournemouth.

Boscombe pier and sands with deckchairs awaiting customers.

Bournemouth Pier at sunset.

16

Bournemouth from Canford Cliffs.

Looking towards Poole Harbour from Canford Cliffs. In the distance are the blue slopes of the Purbeck Hills.

Sandbanks. A lone fisherman waits patiently for a bite at the harbour entrance. In the background is the Haven Hotel where Marconi conducted his first wireless experiments.

The chain ferry which links Sandbanks to Purbeck.

POOLE TO ST ALDHELM'S HEAD

The great natural harbour at Poole has traded with many different nations from time immemorial. The Danes periodically came pillaging and terrifying the inhabitants. Later the Romans landed and started a town at Hamworthy.

Poole itself was a medieval town which grew in importance as Wareham declined with the silting up of the River Frome. The deeper water of Poole Harbour was in any case more suitable for the increasing size of ships and by 1433 it had become the largest port in Dorset. The seventeenth century saw the development of trade with Newfoundland, which brought Poole prosperity for some two hundred years. Trade today takes the form of container ships and a passenger service to the continent. Although the harbour lies above the largest onshore oilfield in Europe, little evidence of it can be seen. BP have gone to great lengths to satisfy environmental concerns.

Now owned by the National Trust, Brownsea is the largest of eight named islands in the harbour. Lord Baden-Powell set up the first Scout camp there in 1907, bringing together boys from greatly differing backgrounds, and at one time over three hundred people were employed in Brownsea's pottery industry. The whole island is very important for wildlife and is famed for its red squirrel population. The northern half of the island is leased to the Dorset Wildlife Trust as a nature reserve.

Beyond the harbour, Shell Bay and Studland Bay together provide Dorset with one of its best beaches, probably the best on the South Coast. Bequeathed to The National Trust by Ralph Bankes, the bays' fine sands and safe bathing make them very popular in summer.

The coast beyond Studland changes dramatically to white chalk cliffs and the shoreline is inaccessible to walkers as far as Swanage. Before it became a delightful little Victorian resort, Swanage was a busy port, shipping out vast amounts of Purbeck stone. It is still a charming place with an extremely good sunshine record, being sheltered on all sides by chalk hills and facing south-east.

At Anvil Point stands the lighthouse, flashing out its nightly warning to shipping. This coast can be dangerous; the sea has claimed many boats and lives here over the years. The shore is accessible only at Dancing Ledge, Seacombe, and Winspit before the west side of St Aldhelm's Head (also called St Alban's Head) is reached.

It was at Renscombe Farm, a short distance inland from St Aldhelm's Head near the village of Worth Matravers, that radar was developed by Sir Robert Watson-Watt and his team of scientists. Their success played a decisive part in Britain's survival in the Second World War.

Finally, the tiny Norman chapel that has stood for over 800 years on the cliff top at St Aldhelm's Head is a tribute not only to the masons who originally built it, but to the remarkable resilience of Purbeck stone.

Boats in Poole Harbour.

Poole Quay at dawn.

Sunset in the harbour.

A wonderful evening afterglow and rising mist in Poole Harbour.

Looking towards the harbour entrance from Godlingston Heath.

Godlingston Heath, west of Studland.

The Agglestone or Holy Stone on Godlingston Heath, with Poole Harbour in the background.

On the River Frome, Wareham.

Studland Bay. Probably the best beach in Dorset, with its silvery sand, dunes giving shelter from the wind and a safe, gently shelving beach.

Little Sea, a nature reserve supporting a vast amount of wildlife, was formed when sand dunes built up and enclosed what is now a freshwater lake.

The only time you can view the white cliffs at Studland from this point is during neap tides.

Handfast Point.

Swanage from Ballard Down.

Swanage beach.

Morning frost on Swanage beach.

Peveril Point from Durlston Head with The Waverley, *the last working paddle-steamer in the UK, just entering Swanage.*

Anvil Point lighthouse has warned mariners of this dangerous coast since 1881.

The remains of one of the small underground quarries at Swanage, with a trolley and a crude hand-operated winding mechanism.

The old quarry workings at Tilly Whim Caves, later used by smugglers. (The name probably comes from Tilly, a Dorset surname, and whim, meaning 'a windlass'.) Once open to the public, the caves are now closed for safety reasons.

The attractive village of Worth Matravers is a popular starting point for walking the Purbeck Hills.

The Coastguard cottages at St Aldhelm's are just visible on the walk down to Seacombe from Worth Matravers.

Corfe Castle. Not quite on the coast, but synonymous with the Isle of Purbeck and stunningly photogenic.

At one time the Swanage railway was responsible for the prosperity of the town but when Beeching deemed it uneconomic, it went the way of many other small branch lines. It has now been revived with the help of volunteers and is thriving once again.

Dancing Ledge. Around the turn of the century, the headmaster of a school at Worth Matravers had this pool blasted out of the rock so his pupils could bathe safely.

Seacombe, like Winspit, is an ideal place to watch the breaking waves – if you don't get too close!

Thrift on the cliff edge at Seacombe provides a splash of colour in early summer.

Winspit in calm weather.

When it is stormy, Winspit is a favourite place to watch the sea crash on to the rocks.

Inside the Norman chapel on St Aldhelm's Head.

St Aldhelm's Head. Sailors treat the turbulent waters below the Head with the utmost respect.

St Aldhelm's Head seen from the west.

54

ST ALDHELM'S HEAD
TO OSMINGTON MILLS

The eighteen miles from St Aldhelm's Head to Osmington Mills are the jewel in Dorset's crown. The sheer grandeur, beauty and variety of this coastline can hardly be equalled in the British Isles. It has witnessed many a wreck over the years and provided numerous places for smugglers to operate, being liberally blessed with caves and coves.

To the west of St Aldhelm's Head is Chapman's Pool, a little bay overshadowed by Houns-tout Cliff and Emmetts Hill. It is generally deserted because of the effort required to walk down to the beach. There is no further possibility of paddling in the sea until Kimmeridge. Strangely, this is a place that has generated little enthusiasm among twentieth-century guidebook writers. Sir Frederick Treves, for example, describes it as 'desolate and dingy' with a 'ridiculous tower on the cliff top', but from a photographic point of view it is one of my favourite locations, the most photogenic site on the coast.

Through its long history many attempts have been made to exploit commercially the shale that is such an intrinsic feature of Kimmeridge. Most have ended in failure, unlike the project to pump very high-grade oil from deep beneath the surface of Kimmeridge Bay. Opened in 1959, the oil well is still in operation. The tower overlooking the bay is called Clavell's Tower after Sir William Clavell, who was knighted by Queen Elizabeth I. It is said that his nephew, who should have gained the title, was denied the honour when he became a highwayman. The marine life within the bay forms the Purbeck Marine Nature Reserve, managed by The Dorset Wildlife Trust.

Beyond Hobarrow Bay and Brandy Bay are Worbarrow Bay and the lost village of Tyneham, taken over by the army during the war — together with a five-mile stretch of Dorset's best coastline — and never returned. As a result of much campaigning, grudging access is now allowed on most weekends and holidays, but within strictly defined limits.

Some years ago I stood looking across Worbarrow Bay and the stunning view of the coast past Arish Mell and Mupe Bay with an old man who had once lived in Tyneham. Indicating what had obviously been a fine Purbeck stone house, he said wistfully, 'I used to live in the most beautiful house in the most beautiful position on the most beautiful bay in England.'

Lulworth Cove is so distinctive that few people will fail to recognise it when shown a picture. Once the sea had broken through the thin wall of limestone at the entrance of the cove, it eroded the softer beds behind, forming an almost perfect circle. It is fascinating to watch the tide coming in on a calm day, creating concentric rings in the cove.

Local folklore has it that before the Battle of Trafalgar, when an invasion was feared, Napoleon came ashore at Lulworth Cove to investigate the possibility of landing an army on the Dorset coast. If there is any truth in the story, it is little wonder that Napoleon thought better of his plan, because this stretch of coastline would be very easy to defend.

Equally popular with visitors is Durdle Door, just a mile west of Lulworth, a huge arch shaped by the sea eroding the softer chalk and leaving the hard limestone. Gulls find the top of the great curve a perfect nesting ground, and I have watched adventurous youths throwing themselves into the sea from at least halfway up the arch.

The coastal path west from Durdle Door is only for the energetic, for it quickly drops to slightly above sea-level to rise again just as steeply a number of times before it reaches the high point of White Nothe, overlooking Ringstead Bay, Weymouth and Portland. Ringstead has its own, usually empty, beach where walkers can paddle and dodge the incoming waves.

Emmetts Hill from St Aldhelm's Head.

Houns-tout Cliff, overlooking Chapman's Pool.

58

From Houns-tout looking west.

From Swyre Head looking west.

Clavell's Tower, now fallen into decay, stands sentinel over Kimmeridge.

The Kimmeridge Ledges – a favourite haunt of windsurfers when the tide is in – look very benign here, but over the centuries they have caused many shipwrecks.

Clavell's Tower from across the bay, bathed in evening sunlight.

Kimmeridge, looking west.

65

*During a cold winter, the little stream that trickles over the cliff at
Kimmeridge freezes, producing this picturesque effect.*

Distant view of Kimmeridge Bay from above the village.

Only one or two boats at Kimmeridge are still used to fish for lobsters.

Bond's Folly, near Creech Grange, donated to the National Trust by J.W.G. Bond,
whose family gave their name to the famous street in London.

Looking back along the coast from Gad Cliff.

From the promontory of the Tout at Worbarrow Bay the impressive view of Gad Cliff and the coast back to Kimmeridge and beyond can be savoured.

Worbarrow Bay. Claimed by many to be the most picturesque bay in England, it has been occupied by the army since the war and public access is restricted.

Looking across Worbarrow Bay to Cockpit Head and Mupe Rocks.

Worbarrow Tout.

Worbarrow Bay in evening sunlight.

*As part of the restoration work carried out by
the Ministry of Defence, Tyneham church (left) has been repaired and the
village is now open to the public.*

*The village of Tyneham was requisitioned by the army during the
Second World War and never returned to the original inhabitants.*

The caves and seclusion of the Mupe area made it attractive to smugglers.

Being just inside the army firing ranges, Mupe Bay is not open all the time and, because of the stiff walk required to reach it, is generally deserted.

Mupe Rocks.

Lulworth Cove. The sea has broken through the hard limestone at the mouth of the bay and eroded the softer rock behind to form this wonderfully romantic circular cove.

Low tide at Lulworth provides many rock pools for children to investigate.

Stair Hole, Lulworth, a miniature Durdle Door created by sea erosion.

St Oswald's Bay in bright summer sunshine.

St Oswald's Bay and Durdle Door seen from Dungy Head.

Rocks at St Oswald's Bay exposed at low tide.

Evening at Durdle Door.

The striking arch of Durdle Door, formed by natural erosion.

The magnificent stretch of undulating coast seen looking east from the summit of White Nothe.

White Nothe. There is a precipitous smuggler's trail down from the summit.

Ringstead Bay from White Nothe.

Ringstead Bay in stormy weather.

The isolation of Ringstead Bay makes it an ideal place to get away from the crowds.

Sheep grazing above Ringstead Bay.

Boulders on the shore at Osmington Mills.

Looking towards Portland from Osmington Mills.

WEYMOUTH AND PORTLAND

In the Middle Ages Weymouth was two separate settlements situated on either side of the river, Melcombe Regis to the north and Weymouth to the south. It was via the former that the Black Death was introduced into England in 1348 by the fleas of infected rats on a boat from the continent. The plague decimated the population and eventually resulted in great social change.

It is George III who has always been given credit for Weymouth's popularity. On the recommendation of a friend he visited the town, liked it and allegedly took his first royal bathe there in his birthday suit. The town became popular even if the mode of bathing did not. To celebrate the royal patronage a huge figure of George III on horseback was carved out of the chalk hill overlooking the harbour. Why he is shown riding away from Weymouth is a mystery. Perhaps it was a subtle symbolic protest at the loss of the American colonies during his reign.

Backed by the grandeur of Dorset's coast, the safe, wide, sweeping, sandy bay makes Weymouth a holiday resort that still entices people to return year after year.

Portland is a huge lump of limestone, approximately four miles long, two miles wide and 500 feet high, bleak and treeless. In 1540 John Leland wrote: 'The people there be good in flinging of stones and use it for the defense of their isle.' The landscape is scarred from centuries of quarrying, which inevitably results in the tipping of a great deal of waste. The demand for Portland stone has fluctuated over the years, but it was the choosing of the stone by Inigo Jones for the Whitehall Banqueting House in 1619 that revived and greatly expanded the industry. Today there is much mechanisation and probably fewer than a hundred workers are employed.

At the southern extremity of the island is Portland Bill, the bare promontory with its two lighthouses looking down on the shoals and rapid currents which are a source of great danger to mariners. Its name is thought to come from the beak-like end of the Isle, described by Harper in *The Hardy Country* as stretching out 'like the head of a bird into the English Channel'.

Like the Isle of Purbeck, Portland erroneously claims island status, although probably with more justification. It is tethered to the mainland only by the long narrow bank of Chesil Beach. In 1830 a bridge was built, making it much easier to cross to and from the island, but before that the short crossing at Small Mouth had to be made by ferry.

In the past, the inhabitants were insular and superstitious and maintained their own customs. For instance, marriage was not entered into until the girl became pregnant, and no one mentioned the word 'rabbit' for fear of bringing bad luck.

Although the Portland naval base has been disbanded, the sound of aircraft can still be heard, because it is from here that the Coastguard's vital Air Sea Rescue helicopters operate, plucking people in trouble from the sea and cliff faces.

The elegant buildings along Weymouth seafront recall the town's historic royal connections.

Weymouth Harbour is a very busy port, catering for fishing boats, leisure craft and a cross-Channel catamaran ferry service.

Weymouth seafront.

Combined air sea rescue exercise involving the RNLI and the Coastguard helicopter.

The fine view of Chesil Beach seen from the top of the island at Portland Heights.

Warm early morning light transforms the bleak stone houses of Fortuneswell.

Abandoned steam engine once used in the quarrying industry.

Church Ope Cove, Isle of Portland. Each beach hut has a little 'garden' of pebbles surrounded by a small wall of pebbles. Pennsylvania Castle and the ruins of Rufus Castle are just visible.

Portland lighthouse, synonymous with the Isle of Portland.

Pulpit Rock. The local young blades think nothing of climbing the rock and throwing themselves into the sea. This father hauled his young son to the top.

THE FLEET TO LYME REGIS

The eight-mile-long Fleet is the largest lagoon in Britain, attracting some of Europe's most unusual wildlife. The Fleet Nature Reserve dates as far back as 1393, when measures were taken to protect its famous colony of mute swans. During the war, Barnes Wallis had his bouncing bomb tested on the waters of the Fleet and a prototype bomb can still be seen in the Abbotsbury Swannery grounds.

Chesil Beach, which guards the southern flank of the Fleet, formed at the end of the last ice age and is composed of pebbles graded in size along its length. It has always been claimed that local fisherman landing on the bank in thick fog could determine exactly where they had landed by the size of the pebbles.

Meade Falkner's famous novel *Moonfleet* is based on the tiny village of Fleet. Only part of the small church there remains, the rest having been washed away during the great storm of 1824, in which an 80-ton sloop was thrown right up on top of Chesil Beach.

Burton Bradstock marks the true end of the Chesil Beach, where the yellow sandstone cliffs appear. The wind and sand have eroded its surface into fantastic shapes like protruding rows of bared teeth.

Sir Frederick Treves' description of West Bay as 'probably the queerest seaport in any part of the British Isles' is rather an exaggeration, although the little harbour is unusual in that it relies on two piers built out into the sea to form a narrow entrance. The River Brit is held back by sluices until low tide, when all the water is released to scour the harbour. During days of good visibility the coast of Devon can be seen to the west, while in the opposite direction the golden sandstone cliffs become an almost incandescent yellow in the evening sunlight.

The South West Coast Path continues beyond West Bay past Eype's Mouth and Seatown, rising up to Golden Cap. At 618 feet, this is the highest sea cliff on the South Coast and provides magnificent views in all directions. It derives its name from the golden crest of upper greensand that glistens in the sunlight or glows in the evening light. To the west it overlooks Charmouth, which Jane Austen loved. She described its 'sweet retired bay, backed by dark cliffs, where fragments of low rock among the sands make it the happiest spot for watching the flow of the tide, and for sitting in unwearied contemplation'.

Just a mile away is Lyme Regis, marking Dorset's western boundary with Devon. It still retains immense character and is the county's gem. Jane Austen stayed in Lyme, which is featured in *Persuasion*, and today the literary connection is continued by John Fowles, who lives in the town. His bestselling novel (later a highly successful film) *The French Lieutenant's Woman* is set in Victorian Lyme.

The discovery in 1811 by the eleven-year-old Mary Anning of an ichthyosaur's skeleton made her famous and the whole area a fossil hunter's paradise. Each erosion of the coast provides an opportunity for fresh discoveries.

1685 was the year of the Duke of Monmouth's landing at Lyme and his ill-fated attempt to claim the throne of England. Some of his recruits who survived the bloody Battle of Sedgemoor faced an even worse fate at the hands of the notorious Judge Jeffreys: several of those convicted of taking part in the Monmouth Rebellion were hanged, drawn and quartered and suspended in baskets for all to see.

In smuggling days Dorset customs-men were much hampered by the peculiar regulations governing the Cobb: ships were allowed to tie up there but the officers had no legal right to examine the cargo until the goods reached the Cobb gate. Naturally, contraband frequently disappeared on that short journey.

Lyme Regis seems an appropriate place to end a visit to this unique county before travelling on into Devon. And, approached from the west, it makes a good appetiser for the delights to come.

Hardy's Monument on Black Down. One of the best viewpoints in Dorset, it commemorates Captain Thomas Masterman Hardy, who served under Admiral Nelson.

The great storm of 1824 destroyed all but the chancel of Fleet church, made famous by Falkner's Moonfleet.

The swans from Abbotsbury Swannery make their home on the Fleet, the largest lagoon in Britain.

Schoolchildren benefit from a natural history lesson given by a member of the Swannery staff.

Abbotsbury and St Catherine's Chapel.

The fifteenth-century tithe barn at Abbotsbury.

116

St Catherine's Chapel on the 250-foot high Chapel Hill from Chesil Beach.

Abbotsbury's sub-tropical gardens are a delight at any time of the year.

Chesil Beach, a graveyard for boats since time immemorial.
Thomas Hardy named it 'Dead Man's Bay'.

West Bexington, a tiny village right on the beach, is a favourite place for fishermen.

121

Burton Bradstock marks the west end of Chesil Beach.

The cliffs at Burton Bradstock, eroded by wind and sea into extraordinary shapes.

East Cliff, West Bay.

West Bay From East Cliff.

125

Rough weather at West Bay.

126

East Cliff at dusk.

The entrance to West Bay harbour takes a pounding during a storm.

The harbour in evening light with a storm brewing.

The distinctive landmark of Colmer's Hill, near Bridport.

Looking east from Doghouse Hill, near Seatown, with a clear view of distant West Bay.

*Until Chideock gets a bypass, all the A35 traffic will
continue to thunder through this ancient little village.*

View from the top of Golden Cap. Seatown is in the foreground and the sandstone cliffs at Burton Bradstock are just visible.

133

Golden Cap from the South West Coast Path, near St Gabriel's.

Golden Cap from Charmouth beach.

The little village of Wootton Fitzpaine nestles in the valley with Portland on the horizon.

Charmouth from Cain's Folly.

Charmouth beach: 'a place to sit in unwearied contemplation' (Jane Austen).

Lyme Regis from Cain's Folly.

Above and opposite: Evening creates a little magic in Lyme harbour.

Lyme Harbour. Three centuries ago it was the fourteenth largest port in Britain.

Lyme Regis retains an old-world charm, probably because its geography makes expansion impossible.